Form a Band!

by Isabel Thomas

Do you want to be in a band?
You need things that do this.

Look in your house. Can you spot things that can help start your band?

Tap

Pans or buckets could be drums.

Hang pan lids up with strings.

Tap the drum kit with a wooden spoon.

Tin cans can be very good drums. Just extend a balloon on to a can.

Tap the balloon with your fingers.
It is the skin of the drum!

Strum

You could turn a box into a box harp. Pick a box with a gap.

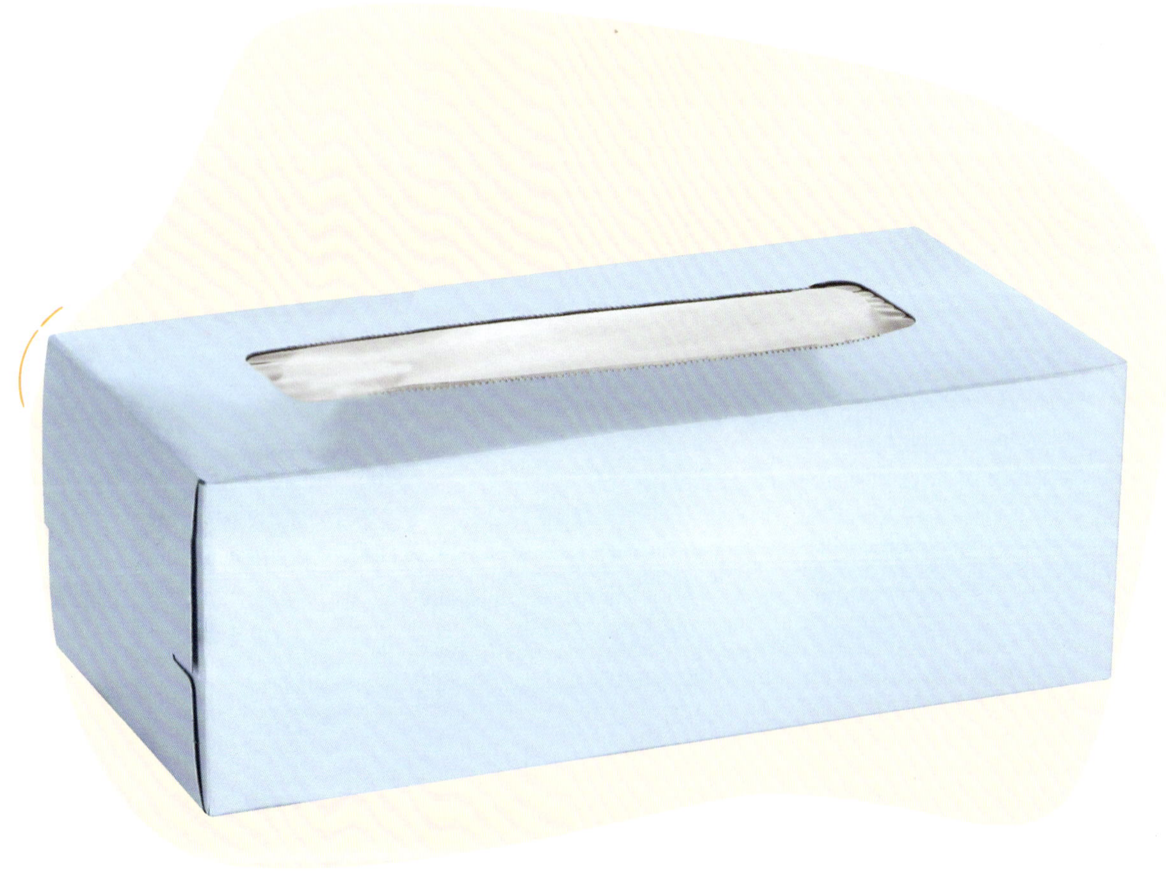

Pull rubber bands across the gap to make strands.

Pop a block under the bands.

Rattle

Do not discard plastic bottles. They could be part of your band!

Put kernels or seeds in the bottle.

Flip the bottle over.

Turn a plastic egg into a maraca.
Put lentils into the egg.

Shut the egg. Stick it between a pair of spoons.

Tap or blow

Put some water in bottles. Tap or blow on the bottles.

Less water will have a low sound.
Lots of water will have a high sound.

Look Back

Encourage students to use the images to review the topic.